Work Smart Not Hard Network Marketers

Series #1: A Guide to Building
Successful IN-Home Sales Organizations

GLENDA BOONE

DEDICATION

To my husband Milton – it's a privilege to share my business, life, and love with you.

To my children Tarin and Lauren– your growth provides a constant source of joy and pride.

To my Mom, Betty, who is a constant source of inspiration.

To my baby sis, Cindy, for always believing and encouraging me that we can conquer the world together.

To my dear friends, Trenia, Ledley and Joan for always supporting my big endeavors.

To all the men and the women of the world who are not afraid to live the life they **WANT** to live!

CONTENTS

Introduction

Webster's dictionary defines passion as…an intense overmastering feeling or conviction; a strong liking or desire for or devotion to some activity, object or concept.

My passion lies in the world of Direct Sales, particularly in Home Sales or what is more commonly known as Home Party Sales.

My Passion for the Home Party Sales Business follows a simple two part design that includes: Good OLE' Mother wit also known as common sense and basic business acumen.

Mother Wit has taught me to remember seven key elements: The Power of Prayer, Purpose, Faith, Encouragement, Persistence, Service and giving Thanks.

Good Business acumen is situated in the R-Pie Theory, which I will discuss later. Now if you will allow me to share my story, you will see how you can also apply my two-part design to follow your passion and turning it into a business.

My story dates back to 1992, when I first began my in home sales consulting career as a Direct Sales Consultant for a widely known Network Marketing Company. A friend of mine invited me to her home for an in-home art viewing and I was quite smitten by the In-Direct Sales Consultant standing in front of me.

To be honest throughout most of the show I was wondering in the back of my mind, "How much money is she making doing this."

I then found myself intrigued by the fact that I realized that I was writing a $500 check for artwork when, before that moment, I did not even know I liked art. As the consultant was completing her sales order and handing me a sales receipt, I raised enough courage to ask her:

"How can I learn to do what you are doing so that I can pay off this large purchase I just made with you?"

We both laughed and then the young lady said something that was profound to me:

"I will make about $750 tonight and this is my second show of the day."

I looked at her and said, oh that's nice. She asked if I would like some information about the company, I told her no, I was too busy, but in the back of my mind I was saying, "I can do this."

After about one week, my beautiful artwork arrived, my husband hung it on the wall and I thought to myself once again, "I can do this" but, I let the moment pass.

The very next day, I received a nice post card in the mail from my In-Direct Sales Consultant thanking me once again for the purchase and letting me know that she had another great week and to contact her if I ever decided to join the team.

I started speaking to self once more saying, "Self you can do this". But, once again I let the moment pass. For 2 months I received a post card in the mail from my In-Direct Sales Consultant updating me on her progress, and then it happened. My car died, and I needed to earn more money, who do you think I called?

Not only was she elated that I called her, she told me that she was waiting for the call and she believed I had everything it took to be successful in this business. You know what, she was right my very first year in the business I produced $500,000 in sales and established a national direct sales network that consisted of more than 200 individuals. Life was good or so I thought,

In 1994, I met Mr. Larry "Poncho" Brown, who enlightened me that the Direct Sales Company by which I was employed (full time at that point) was partaking in the plagiarism of African American Visual Artists artworks.

For many who may be unfamiliar with the term of plagiarism as it relates to artwork, I'll give you an example:

For many years, African American art was not considered a major commodity. In fact, it was with the help of people like Bill Cosby and Oprah Winfrey who allowed African American Artists to utilize their TV shows as platforms to showcase their works.

Shortly thereafter, large publishing houses began to realize that not only was African American Art a commodity, it was also a virtually untapped market.

We must understand the context by which this travesty occurred you see in those days, there was no face book, Twitter, or Instagram; so many great African American Artists were forced to peddle the artwork from the streets during summer festivals or out the trunks of their cars.

As the demand for African American Artists works grew, large publishing houses set out to capitalize off this new found untapped market, yet, instead of going to the artist direct and negotiating reproduction deals, many publishing houses simply paid emerging artists, many living abroad, to duplicate the African American Artist original works, thereby cutting out the artist, aka (middleman).

In an attempt to avoid confusion, by pass copyright laws and to present and added value to the public, publishing houses transferred a paper image onto canvas giving the perception that their works were of higher value and created by a totally different artist.

This practice generated millions of dollars each year into the visual arts industry, yet African American Artist were still marketing their works from the trunks of their cars or at state fairs.

That's were Pray, Purpose and Faith-the first three elements of Mother Wit-lead me to take action.

In 1994, after my meeting with Mr. Brown, I, with the support of my husband, Milton, invested our entire savings and created the Black Heritage Visual Arts Marketing Corporation, together we set out with our mission to go into homes with a goal of educating the public of the travesty that was occurring and offer representation of the artists works at the same time. In essence we started our own Direct Sales Art Consulting Organization.

This friend was no easy feat, but through encouragement from dear friends and unlikely sources, we remained true to our passion and pressed on with conviction.

When I got down, I took the time to think about how two of my personal inspirations, Oprah Winfrey and Halle Berry weathered their own private struggles and professional obstacles to become the successful women that they are today.

In fact, one of my most memorable moments is when I had the opportunity to meet Oprah Winfrey briefly at the New York Fine Art Show. Oprah encouraged me to follow my dream no matter what, and told me that if she can do it so can I and by 1995, persistence-the fourth element-paid off.

Milton and I reached out to the most acclaimed African American artist in the country and within one year we had a roster of more than 40 artists that donated the inventory and 100 In-Home Sales Consultants that we trained literally to travel around one home at a time with a focus on educating rather than selling.

In February 1995, we held our first public Black Heritage Art Show in Baltimore, Maryland it was a huge success PR wise and a big bust financially, but that was ok, because it put us on the map and gave us credibility in the eyes of African American Artists, the public and even the large publishing houses.

In fact in 1996, those large publishing houses that were once stealing the artists works, had no choice but to contact African American Artists direct if they wanted to sell African American Art to the public because Black Heritage Visual Arts opened the public eyes and their jig was up!

Now, we separated ourselves from our competition, the public knew that we were deeply rooted in the community, and projected a passion to educate and not just sell, we gained total support of African American visual artists and art collectors alike. It was a huge blessing for us and because of this we felt the need to give back and be of service.

Service is the Fifth Element:

You see, in life we are all given gifts and passions and we should use them to uplift others. This reminds me of an old church song that says, "If I can Help Somebody along the way, then my living shall not be in Vain."

After successfully establishing our own Direct Sales/Network Marketing Company it was time to give back and be of service to others. Hence, Milton and I established the Heritage Awards Ceremony a nationally exposed African American Contemporary visual arts recognition ceremony. The Heritage Awards Ceremony recognized the achievements of contemporary African American Visual Artists and generated recognition by the mainstream art galleries, organizations and corporations.

That same year, we established the African American Visual Arts Association a 501 c-3 nonprofit organization that offers educational seminars, youth arts competitions, scholarships, youth art camps, exhibition space, financing and exposure for emerging artists.

Finally, Mother Wit has taught me to be appreciative-and in all things give thanks. So today, as in all days, I thank God and then I thank those who have helped me along the way.

Remember earlier, I mentioned, the R-Pie-Theory.

Well. All R-Pie theory stands for is Research, Planning Implementation and Evaluation.

Any good business idea begins with research, so research, research, and research! Familiarize and check references of companies you are you are planning to partner with BEFORE you sign the contract.

Do your research, find out about the industry, training, commission structure, hidden fees and any required certifications, and understand that there are a lot of great companies but there are also a lot of scams.
RESEARCH!!!

Next, remember to plan carefully and be sure to plan in increments- list your short term and long-term goals. Write them down, pin them up on your mirror each day.

Once you get the plan, it then becomes time to implement. I see so many In Home Sales Consultants fail at this point because they never can get out of the planning stage. The plan is NEVER going to be perfect. At some point you have to set things in motion.

Finally, the last ingredient for the pie is to EVALUATE.

Evaluate as you go along by setting benchmarks, for example if your plan calls for you to conduct 2 parties per week to achieve your goals, did you implement it?

It is also good to evaluate whether or not that goal is achievable for you at this point of your life, if it's not, be true to yourself and your business, own up to it and get out, don't waste your time and don't waste your sponsor's time.

Many persons like yourselves have purchased this book because they know that they are full of potential and have a desire and passion to do this business; however they also feel that they don't have the necessary marketing and training tools to help keep them productive in the Direct in Home Sales market place.

Would you say that's a fare assessment of how you feel?
☐Yes ☐No

If you answered yes, you made a wise decision by investing in this guide to help take your business to the next level. This book will list for you the most successful marketing strategies used for building and maintaining a successful IN Home Direct Sales Network. The fluff has been removed and the system proven with a variety of networking marketing companies. It doesn't matter if you are selling nutritional products, jewelry or candles, if the basic foundational steps are followed you will be a success!

Rest assured, you are full of potential and now that you are ready to fulfill your goals, the next step is to begin implementing the marketing strategies highlighted in this guide as they will surely help you fulfill your destiny!

NOW, LET'S GET STARTED IN BUILDING YOUR FUTURE!

IT ALL STARTS WITH YOU

- ENTHUSIASM

- CONSIDERATION

- SINCERITY

- APPRECIATION

- APPEARANCE

- SELF-ORGANIZATION

- PROFESSIONALISM

- PREPARATION

- CONFIDENCE

- FUN

- SERVICE AND FOLLOW-UP

- MOTIVATION

Every successful Direct Sales Consultant will share the same secret with you:

"YOUR SUCCESS OPERATING IN DIRECT SALES DEPENDS SOLELY ON YOU!

If you really want to make a full time career as a network marketer operating in Direct Sales you must develop an "I Can" attitude; "I Love" personality "I am successful" appearance and finally, you must:

Become a master at creating the ultimate In Home Party/show/event.

I know, what you are thinking, 'Yea right, that is easier said than done'. Well, my fellow colleagues, I submit to you that I used a plan of action that within two years, had created a 2 million dollar sales organization ranging from the East to West Coast netting me a $5,000 override check every month as well as an additional $3,000 personal sales check. I was in heaven, making a decent living doing what I loved to do with people I loved associating with. To me back at that time I considered that making crazy money without having to work hard, just smart.

Most of the highly paid people in direct sales companies are the consultants/independent distributors and you want to know why? There is very low overhead costs associated with being an owner of a Network Marketing Organization.

Unlike owning a Network Marketing Company, developing Network Marketing organizations within companies is one of few business' one can establish where the cost to start up is now a days, less than the cost of a smart phone. So, if you are wondering if you can build a successful Direct Sales organization in this economy, absolutely you can, if you are willing to follow a proven system.

I used GB's Plan of Action system to help me build a very profitable business and elevate me to the level by which I now serve in this industry. For those of you who really want to become successful building successful Network Marketing or Direct Sales organization, get your pens and pencils ready because what you are about to learn will change the course of your business and hopefully life forever.

Chapter 2

FOCUS ON MOVING PRODUCT
NOT
RECRUITING PEOPLE

When one decides to join a network marketing company many times network marketers place their emphasis on building the organization from the onset rather than focus on moving product. I would argue that moving product is more important. Focusing your sales force on moving products allow network marketers within the organization opportunities to obtain leads that will lead to people who will be interested in the organization's business opportunity.

There are several strategies being used today to move company products including, online marketing, promotional flyers, public events and word of mouth. Yet, I have found the most successful and sustainable way is to move product and recruit is via In-Home Parties/Presentations/Shows. The In Home direct sales approach has been proven for many years by most successful Network Marketing Companies, Why? Because it works! Those most successful at mastering this system are those that:

Set Goals

In order to move your company's product, you must set goals and the key element to achieve one's goal is to have **DESIRE**!

Desire must be created and maintained by two individuals in order to achieve the goal of moving product in the In Home Direct Sales industry.

A. Yourself

B. The Hostess

Creating Desire in Yourself!

A. Believe In Yourself

What do you see yourself accomplishing from your In Home Sales Career?

Do you believe you can accomplish what you have listed above?

☐Yes   ☐No

Why?

_____
_____
_____
_____
_____
_____
_____
_____ .

If you answered yes to the above, type out your answers and keep them posted on a mirror that you use each morning and each night. If you answered no, please discontinue this reading and continue to work your full time job!

Belief in yourself and faith in God will create Desire for you to become a successful In Home Sales Consultant.

B. Goal Setting

What are your short-term goals?

_____

_____

_____

_____:

What are your long-term goals?

_____

_____

_____

_____:

Goals serve as the road map for us to achieve what we desire

Creating Desire in the Hostess

a. The hostess biggest fears are:

1. Nobody will come

2. Nobody will buy

How did you feel when you hosted your first In Home party?

_____
_____
_____
_____
_____
_____
_____.

If you have never hosted a party, stop don't sign the contract to become a consultant until you host at least one in-home sales party. You don't want to get into something that you can't commit to 100%. So many people write a check only to find it was much more work than they bargained for.

How did you feel when your family and friends received their e-vites and starting calling and texting bombarding you with questions that you could not answer?

_____
_____
_____
_____
_____.

Did you hold your show on the original scheduled date or did you reschedule your party?

☐Yes   ☐No

You build Desire in the hostess by building the relationship!

It is the enthusiasm and professionalism that you project that will lay the groundwork for a successful In Home Party. The time you spend guiding your hostess is usually directly related to the success of your show and the number of possible recruit leads you will obtain. You build a relationship by:

A. Reassurance.

B. Relieving your hostess of her biggest fears which are what? _____

And: _____

Were you excited after speaking with your consultant for the first time about your In Home Show?

☐Yes   ☐No

Did you immediately begin completing your guest list after you spoke to your hostess?

☐Yes   ☐No

Remember:

You are the professional and this is your business, not the host/hostess. The goal you set for your In Home parties are yours and yours alone, not the host/hostess.

The host/hostess goal is to earn free or drastically reduced product. Thus, realizing this as a direct sales consultant, you know that in order to reach your goal and let's put a number out there of $500.00 min. retail sales, you must create and maintain the hostess desire level at all times to get her/him free or discounted merchandise.

If the hostess appears unmotivated at the beginning of hostess coaching, you will have to continue to build his/her desire, you accomplish this goal by asking questions:

1. You informed me when you booked the party that you really wanted ----------merchandise, do you still want that merchandise?

2. _____Do you have enough confidence in me to believe that I am a professional and trust that I will get the sales needed to obtain the merchandise you desire for free or at 50% discount rate if you follow my plan of action?

**Remember you are now building the hostess desire, which is to get free merchandise, and or deep discounts. Keep him/her focused on their goal by building their desire to get what they want so that you can get the right people to the party which will generate at least $500.00 in retail sales and create the opportunity for you to obtain recruit leads! **

Keep your host/hostess excited or reschedule his/her party!

It is always more beneficial for you to reschedule a show as opposed to having a cancellation. Reschedule translates into an open lead for you at a later time. Cancellation means the party's over with no sales and no recruit leads!

C. Follow a proven plan of action

Do you follow a **proven** plan of action now?

☐Yes   ☐No

How consistent are you at following it?

_____

_____ .

CHAPTER 3
GB'S PLAN OF ACTION

Creating an Ideal Guest List—leads of your future

1. Coaching Your hostess through unexpected anxieties—
Holds your show together

2. Client Calling: Take what your clients want to see and
sell more

3. The Party: Achieving the hostess desires—meeting your
goals

The Guest List:

Create the Guest List you want to have never assuming
your hostess knows neither what you want nor what your
need to do your job!

How did you feel when you received your electronic guest
list form?

_____

_____.

What was your reaction to seeing 40 lines of requested E-
mail addresses?

_____

_____.

Did you begin filling out your guest list immediately?

☐Yes   ☐No

Did you complete a guest list at all?

☐Yes   ☐No

How many people attended your party? _____

What was your party's total sales? (Not including hostess gifts or purchases) _____

Developing and maintaining great Guest Lists is the Key to building a successful In Home Sales business, it is your business lifeline. It will help you to book shows, recruit people and build a very strong sales network. If you fail to learn the importance, purpose and use of a hostess guest list properly, you will not succeed in this business.

Many In Home sales consultants fail because they do not learn the importance of this tool. Many don't even use this tool and often wonder why sales are low and they can't recruit. In order to successfully use this tool you must assist your hostess in completing this list: As when you have a perfect guest list, you create high sales which creates referrals that ensures steady income for your business.

The perfect guest list consist of at least 40 people in different categories including:

1. Work Colleagues

2. Church Members

3. Hair Stylists

4. Insurance Agents

5. Teachers or day care providers

6.Neighbors

7. Significant other's (SO) colleagues

8. SO hair stylists/barbers/work colleagues

9. Doctors

10.Family members and Friends

It is important to complete the guest list is this order every time. (More on this a little later in the chapter)

Notice, I listed family members and friends last, because this group will often come to the party to support you, but definitely won't have a problem not making a purchase. Why you may ask? Well, because they are your close family and close friends so they realize that you won't be upset with them for long if they don't make a purchase.

If the Direct Sales Consultant depends on the host/ hostess to invite guests on his or her own to the show without a roadmap and some direction, the hostess will surely invite mostly family and close friends into their home, which in turn, will not help the host or hostess in getting what they want which is free/discounted merchandise. If the host/hostess does not get what they want, and they will not think of you as a professional and your chances of that host/hostess recommending or assisting you move more product in the future will become slim to none.

Without recommendations, referrals and admiration, you will not be able to book parties and if you don't host in-home-parties/presentations/shows in the direct sales industry, you will not be able to recruit and if you are not able to recruit and you are a network marketer, your business will die. Maybe a slow death, but it will die because you will begin to lack motivation, which will cause you to lose your **DESIRE!**

Further, leaving the host/hostess out there alone will allow too much opportunity for the hostess to believe that his/her party wont' be a success which will make them lose their desire to want your products anymore which will cause a cancellation.

Finally many consultants believe because they penciled in a party on their calendar it is a confirmed party, that is not the case, you do not have a confirmed party on your calendar until the hostess gives you back a completed guest list, only then should you assume you have a confirmed party and not just a party lead.

If you want to cut corners in your plan of action completing the host/hostess guest list is not a step that you want to miss. Although it may be time consuming it is the most important part of building your Direct Sales Network Organization, you will learn why shortly.

TIP: As the professional, you are in control of your calendar not the hostess and you don't have a confirmed party until you have a guest list in your hand. All the bookings on your calendar book are simply party leads. Remember this key point at all times, No guest, list No Party!

Hostess Coaching

If you are successfully working this business, you should be able to book at least 3 parties at each party and obtain minimum retail sales of at least $500. Mastering the Hostess Coach System will assist you in achieving this goal and ensure your business continuous growth.

Hostess Coaching allows you to build the hostess desire as well as monitor your calendar to ensure the party will hold and achieve your goals. During this phase of the plan of action the in home Sales Consultant is building his/her professionalism by proving to the hostess and clients that he/she knows what they are doing and there is nothing for the host/hostess to worry about. Hostess coaching consist of 4 phone calls.

1. Reassurance and mailing/emailing/face booking of the guest list

2. Coaching the hostess on responding to rejection and objections

3. Client calling

4. Reminder Calls

Reassurance and mailing of guest list

1. Reassure your hostess that you are a professional, you know what you are doing and your goal is to help them get what they want. In order to do that, you have a proven plan of action that they agree to follow.

a. Help them fill out the guest list while you have them on the phone in the order in which you need. (according to the perfect guest list tips offered in previous chapters)

b. Reassure them they are going to have a wonderful show

c. Remind them of their goals

Coaching the Hostess on Handling Objections and Declines

Every host/hostess will become nervous when they check their e-vite list or voice mail only to hear people are not coming. You want to let the host/hostess know before the calls starts coming their way that rejects are going to happen, assuring them that it is a normal process. You want to inform your host/hostess that:

a. The goal is to have a few persons at their home that will be interested in the product and make a purchase. The goal is NOT to have a houseful of people to entertain for the evening. Assure the hostess again that you are the professional and feel very confident in the fact that she will have a great party and inform the host/hostess that it is a good thing that people call to decline as that helps you the professional in preparing for the party.

b. Ask the host/hostess not to attempt to answer any questions related to the products but assure them that the consultant will be giving them a personal call to give them a little more detail regarding the product. Ask them to only give a testimony as to why they are hosting the party and how much they love the product and really want them to try it out.

c. Coach host/hostess on how to respond to decline by advising them they certainly understand that their schedule won't allow them to come and that his/her consultant will be calling them direct to allow them the opportunity to learn more about the product and the opportunity to still make a purchase online on the hots/hostess behalf as their online book purchase will be credited to his/her account.

d. Reassure them they are going to have a wonderful party

e. Remind them of their goals

Guest Calling (Dialing for dollars)

You have two goals in mind when calling the guests from a host/hostess guest list that are:

a. to advise them of the host/hostess expectation of the presence and purchase and;

b. Create the guests desire to want to come and make a purchase.

You can accomplish these goals by:

Asking questions!

a. What type of artwork do you have in your home right now? Traditional or contemporary?

b. What type of nutritional products do you currently use? Liquid or pill?

c. What style of jewelry do you normally like to wear?

d. What type of coffee do you prefer caffeinated or decaffeinated?

e. What type of Makeup foundation do you prefer liquid or powder?

The purpose of asking these questions is to find out what type of products each guest will be interested in sampling at the party and to build a relationship with the guest just as you have accomplished with the host/hostess. Your goal is to leave an impression with each guest that you are really a professional and to begin building their desire so that they will feel like they will miss something if they don't attend.

For Example, Let's say that I am conducting a party as a direct sales make up consultant for a hostess by the name of Lynn. I helped Lynn complete her guest list and now I am at the point where I need to call the guest list to find out who is coming.

Most important to remember in this step is that you are trying to figure out for your hostess who will be attending, where their interest lies and pre-sell products to the attending guests have expressed interest. You will accomplish this goal by educating the guest about the product over the phone before the party.

It is crucial to advise each confirmed guest that you will make sure to bring that product to the party just for them. At that point in the telephone conversation, the guest usually will say either "great" or "I am not going to be able to attend" with a suggested response being:

"Wow I am so sorry that you won't be able to attend, however, that is not a problem for Lynn because we have a catalog and website portal that I can direct you via email tonight, you can visit our website and make your order and Lynn will get credit for the sale. Let me just confirm your email address as….. "

Guest says ok, I end the call by ensuring the guest that I will let Lynn know that she will not be able to attend but will make a purchase on her behalf.

*This my friends, is the way to ensure you don't have to worry about making sales at a party, because your are now building the clients desire to come and have planted a seed of what they plan to purchase.** In essence you can pretty much approximate what your minimum sales will be before the party is even held.

Once you complete your guest calls, you should immediately contact the hostess and advise her of the names of people that confirmed as well as notify her of the people who declined but committed to make a purchase. The major point to keep in mind during this part of the hostess coach process is to **NOT ALLOW THE HOSTESS TO ENSURE GUESTS ARE COMING, YOU ARE THE PROFESSIONAL, ITS ALL UP TO YOU!**

Reminder Calls:

Call the confirmed guests 24 hours before the party to remind each guest of hostess excitement about their attendance at her party and your expectation of meeting him/her on _____date at _____time. Then:

a. Reassure guest that they are going to have a great time at the party

b. Remind guest that you are going to bring the items they noted they may be interested in to the party

Why do you think making reminder calls will increase the attendance of the host/hostess party/show?

_____

_____

_____

_____.

At what point do you think the hostess begins showing some form of commitment to having the party/show?

_____

_____

_____

_____.

When does the consultant realize the party/show will hold?

_____

_____

_____

_____

_____.

CHAPTER 4
WORKING YOUR GUEST LIST TO RECRUIT

In the previous chapter, I mentioned the importance of helping a host/hostess complete his/her guest list noting how it can provide an excellent source of lead generators for future sales. Let me explain how.

As you may recall, in the previous chapter I stressed the crucial need to complete the guest list a certain way every time and that is because you are actually categorizing your future lead system. For instance, the first group of people on the perfect guest list is co-workers. Co-workers always make the best group of people to call on to host parties. You see co-workers are very competitive, they will agree to host a party and purchase product because they don't want to be outdone by other co-workers present.

Maintaining a strong pipeline of leads determines how fast a network marketing organization will grow. Leads keeps the product sales flowing through the pipeline. and the best leads can only be obtained by conducting in home shows or direct sales events.

I prefer in home parties/shows as they allow me to build a guest list from a relationship I developed with a host/hostess that I can use for both additional party/show leads as well as recruiting leads.

The perfect guest lists becomes your saving grace, when you need parties/shows and you have run out of your initial circle of family members and friends. You simply refer to their guests list and call the first group of people on the guest list.

In addition, guest list also serve as great recruiting tools. You may recall I mentioned that Teachers/daycare providers, insurance agents and hair stylists are persons who are not afraid to speak publicly, hence, when you are trying to recruit and when the well runs dry, no problem, pull out the guest list and call those group of individuals. If you learn to use the perfect guest list as a tool you will never run out of prospects and you will never have to worry about not having any party/show leads. They are there, you just have to work them. After you complete the educating process at the show, your focus should then be on recruiting the people you have built a relationship with over the phone. Let's learn how in the next chapter.

CHAPTER 5
BUILDING A SUCCESFUL SALES ORGANIZATION

Many in home Sales Consultants fail at their business because they don't take the time to master the art of recruiting. Statistics show that the average sales life of an in Direct Sales Consultant is three years. However, the average sales career of a In Home Sales Manager is 5 years or more and a Director 8 years or more. Why such a short career span for a in home sales consultant?

They grow tired of selling and they rarely earn enough money to realize their dream, which in most cases is to retire from their full time careers and manage their in home sales business on a full time basis.

If you want to be an entrepreneur in the In Home Sales Industry, you **MUST** learn to master the art of recruiting, building and managing a down line. It's really quite a simple process; the hard part is following the strategy. Let's look at each one of the necessary strategies needed to be successful at building a down line organization.

Maintain a Database of Recruit Prospects.

After training more In-Home Sales Consultants during my career and attending more training events than one can ever imagine, I realized one of the main problems consultants faced was their focus at the home show stayed on sales and not on recruiting.

Many consultants failed to remember that once they entered into the host/hostess home, sales were already accounted for (If they were following GB's proven plan of action, that is) If you follow your company's plan of action, people will know that you expect them to buy at the party and will have some idea of what they are looking for! Hence, your goal once you arrive at the party is to reintroduce the products you already spoke to the guests about when you spoke to them earlier in the process, at this stage once the guest views and test the product they are either going to buy it or not buy it.

You have done all the legwork to ensure sales; now it's time to shine and show everyone how wonderful your career is and find those people who want to associate themselves with you.

People desire to associate with people they perceive as being successful!

Do you present yourself as confident and successful at your shows?

☐**Yes**   ☐**No**

Do you look for people who are looking at you like "I can do that?"

☐**Yes**   ☐**No**

Do you ask people to join your business?

☐Yes   ☐No

Why or Why not?

_____

_____

_____

_____

_____.

Here are three people who attend every show that would make great In Home Sales Consultants:

1. Mr./Mrs. Can I help you with that?

2. Mr./Mrs. know it/have it all/ Oh, I know that artist, oh I have that piece…

3. Mr./Mrs. Butt in, (You can't finish your presentation because they are butting in…)

Do not become bothered by these types of guests as it is these types of individuals that become your future recruits. Their annoying actions during your presentation is simply their way of letting you know that they like what they see and may want to do what you do!

We will talk a little more about recruiting later on in the book, but I would like to share a couple of really nice tips with you regarding recruiting:

Show them the Money!

Always take a copy of your highest paycheck to your In Home Part/Show. When Mr./Mrs. Butt- in starts talking, tell them that you think they would make a great consultant than share with them how you are serious and pull out a copy of your most recent (highest) commission check and let them pass it around the room. I guarantee before the end of the night at least 2 people will come up to you to learn more about becoming a sales consultant.

Implement an Electronic Stay in Touch System

Always place Mrs. Can I help, Mr. I know/have it all, and Mrs. Butt in on the e-stay-in-touch system. (See below)

There are two things an In Home Sales Consult must learn to do in order to keep the jellybean jar full.

a. Set up a face book fan page for your business, then at some point in your presentation at each home show ask all the guest to pull out their smart phones and like your fan page. If you have twitter or Instagram, now is the time to get and stay connected to possible recruits.

b. Obtain the guests email addresses and create a subscriber list so that you can stay in touch.

Staying in touch with people who attended the party/presentation/show is crucial for recruiting purposes.

Make a point to every week to send an e-post card to your recruit leads and commit to doing this for at least 16 consecutive weeks. I assure you that you will receive a phone call with a request a request to block them from your distribution list or a response noting, "I am ready to join."

A word of caution here, if you start this system you have to keep it up because as soon as you stop staying in touch, your lead could very easily join under another sales consultant or possibly, call into your company's headquarters and you, my friend, will be devastated. (I am just saying)

Here are some examples of what you can write to your prospects

Week 1

Dear Belinda.

I had a great weekend. I conducted two In Home shows spent a total of 4 hours working at my shows and earned $750 that will pay my car note. It can pay yours too, call me.

Glenda.

Week 2

Dear Belinda,

Me again, had another great weekend, conducted 2 shows and $1000 think I'll go on a vacation. I hope you will be able to join me one day, call me.

Glenda

Week 3

Dear Belinda:

I am so sorry I haven't heard from you yet. Are you still thinking how great it might be owning your own business? I only had one show this weekend because I wanted to spend some time with my family. Made $300 for 2 hours of work, call me….

You get it!

Keeping Track of your leads

You should formulate a lead-tracking sheet to keep track of each prospect that responds to your stay in touch system. This sheet should include their personal information and dates listing the last time that you were in contact with them.

TIP: At some point you might want to send them a personal note card in the mail. Nothing beats a handwritten personal note when attempting to build sustainable relationships.

CHAPTER 6
INVITE AND INVEST

Every Network Marketer interested in working smart not hard should develop a method by which they master capturing the attention and desire of recruiting prospects to assimilate into their organization as well as maintaining the desire and motivation of recruits already affiliated within their organization.

I have found in my many years of experience, that the most productive way to achieve these objectives is by investing time, money and resources to develop successful weekly meetings, webinars and social gatherings. These encounters should be:

- Highly Energetic

- Motivational

- Accountable

- Productive

- FUN!!!

These tasks work best with the assistance of other in Network Market builders whose goals and objectives are similar to that of your own as it will require an investment of serious time, and money. You will NOT build sustainable organizations by only gifting product-oriented investments to your down-line organization. (another secret network marketers working smart not hard rarely share Beware and be ready as this strategy will cost you some dough, however your personal investment and consistent contact with your organization is crucial, it allows you to:

- Motivate existing recruits

- Recognize recruits within the organization who are staying on track

- Hold recruits in your organization that is falling short of their personal goal.

- Teach new recruits your company's plan of action

- Duplicate yourself

Don't just have meetings, conference calls and accountability checks, strive for productive, fun and motivational encounters. You have to make it "I can't miss this event kind of evening!"

I can remember when I was starting in the network marketing business, I hated going out to the weekly meetings hosted by my up line because they were so boring. We did the same thing over and over again. We never learned anything new and many people in our group felt that it was a waste of time. Hence, practically everyone stopped coming out to the weekly meeting. I, however, had so much passion to succeed in the business that I asked my up line if I could invest some money and invite someone into our meeting. I offered to pay the expenses of bringing a motivational speaker in and assured my up line that I would fill the hotel room space that she was wasting money on each week. She agreed, I set out to invite as many In-Home Sales Consultants as I could. Then, I went to my recruit prospect list and began inviting all of my recruiting prospects and asked those in my down line to do the same. In those days we sent e-mails and or mailed letters (old-school-as there was no face book or e-vite system in place at that time)

That letter included a bio and a very nice flyer of the person that we was going to speak and required a RSVP for them to attend.

Needless to say, the meeting was a huge success, more than 200 people were in attendance, many In-Home Sales Consultants including myself, recruited persons that night and my up line learned how to run a energetic, motivational weekly meeting. After the meeting, we took our guest to dinner and picked her brain! (Of course I asked my upline to foot that bill.) Not only did our meetings become more productive, many people in our organization began to build their own organizations and now felt a need to support and attend the weekly meetings, which helped us cut the cost as the organization grew our individual cost decreased.

I cannot stress enough the importance of attending a weekly meeting, conference call or webinar if they are motivational and productive. Remember, as a network marketer who has made the decision to build an organization, you must be willing to invest in these meetings and or social gatherings to ensure that they are beneficial to your recruits and thereby will be profitable to you. If your up-line meetings are not motivational fun and productive, do not set yourself and your group up for failure, duplicate your own using a successful formula because these forums are a must if you are to succeed.

I would suggest that you share in the expense and split the workload of managing weekly meetings and please by all means invite speakers in to help everyone, including yourself, learn a few tricks of your trade.

CHAPTER 7
SPEND MONEY TO MAKE MONEY

When you decide to begin building a sales organization, you must be willing to invest some of your funds in promotion campaigns. These campaigns help to keep your recruits motivated. Everyone will get use to receiving their retail sales and commission check, yet no one ever tires of being recognized individually and receiving a gift for their hard earned efforts. Most network marketers make the mistake and wait for headquarters to host their annual conferences to motivate their sales organizations, however, based on my experience, if you wait that long to motivate recruits, you will lose ½ of your sales force.

People are motivated by recognition more than they are money. Invest in airline tickets to anywhere in the country (normally around $300 if you go on Airtran or Southwest) or small weekend getaways to start off, but do plan to spend some of your manager's earnings on promotional campaigns for your down line.

Invest in company sponsored event tickets as promotional giveaways to your business partners. Let's face it, going to companywide conferences are expensive to say the least. I am sure members of your team would appreciate an opportunity to earn a paid in full annual conference trip, think about how many members will be working hard for a chance at that benefit. Not only will the group be moving more product, each will earn more money, which will help them get what they want , which moves you closer to having everything you want. "Invest and Invite" is working smart not hard!

CHAPTER 8
DUPLICATE, DUPLICATE
AND DUPLICATE AGAIN!

If you want to build a successful sales organization, teach your down line the process of duplication. Teach them everything that you do. Go to a party and **show** them how to do a party as they watch you present on their behalf and gift them with the total sales and commission (invest). **Show** them how to prospect for recruits while at the party and **show** them how to host successful weekly meetings. Most Network Marketers do show their recruits how to book and hold parties and events by hosting one day in home or office trainings, but the buck stops there. They don't **show** them how to do what they do. The point I really want to drive home here **is don't tell them, Show them!!!!** I am sure you all heard the famous saying, "I Can Show You much better than I can TELL you." Teach them by process of duplication and you will be a success.

Don't just talk a good game!

The fastest way to lose a recruit is to tell them to do something that you are not doing. There is no way that a recruit will believe that you can show them how to be successful and they never see your name highlighted in the company's newsletter. You must lead by example to be successful at building an organization.

Know your company's policies and procedures inside and out!

Your will surely lose some of your new recruits respect if you are unfamiliar with the company's policies and procedures. They will question everything that you say and do if you appear to them as being unprepared or not know what you are doing.

Engage in a refresher course with your manager if you are weak in any area of your company's training program.

Help Your New Recruit to "Kick-Start Their Business" and Build using a Show and Tell Approach

In Home Sales Consultants are fortunate! They don't have to be limited to just scheduling In Home parties. The best way to help your new recruit get started in this business is to show and encourage them to use the company's catalog or direct them to your web portal. I named this program: Show and Tell. Your company's catalog and or web portal serves as a lead generator for your new recruit and YOU!

If you train recruits to show their catalog everyday or share their website link to four people, they will generate either a recruit lead or a sale.

In Home Sales Consultants across the country have used my 4 a-day-Show-and-Tell-Plan to get their business off to a great start. Show your catalog or website portal four times a day and let your prospects tell you what they want!

Example #1 Co Workers:

Scene for Role Play (advise your New Recruit to picture themselves at work seated across from a co-worker.

INSC: Cindy, I recently became an In Home Sales Consultant and wanted to share with you some of the products I market that I think you would definitely be interested in. I'd like you to take a couple minutes to review my catalog or visit my website. (Lay catalog on her desk, or pull up your website portal on their desktop.)

Cindy: Oh wow, these are nice!

IHSC: Which one do you really like?

Cindy: There are so many!

IHSC: I know.... well why I don't give you a couple of minutes to narrow down your selections and I'll be happy to assist you with your order.

Cindy: These are nice BUT...I DON'T HAVE ANY MONEY!

IHSC: I completely understand not everyone has disposable income these days; however, you can receive what you want for free or at a great discount just by hosting a show. (Party-event-whatever term your company uses)

Cindy: I DON'T HAVE ANY LUCK HOSTING SHOWS.

IHSC: Oh...if you really feel that you would not have a successful show, then maybe you might be interested in doing a book (online) show for me by sharing with some of our co-workers and your family members?

Cindy: Oh, well, I guess I can do that, becoming a Direct Sales Consultant with your company sounds interesting, is it an expensive business to get into?

IHSC: Funny you should mention that because I was just thinking how great this business might be for you to earn some extra money or maybe even start a whole new career? To answer your question it is not an expensive business to get involved with at all when you consider the cost of owning one's own business. I'll be happy to go over the career opportunity with you but it is easier if I show you. I am available to do shows next month on the following dates _____and _____which would be a better day for you to host a show, earn free product and see how easy it is to earn a great supplemental income? Now don't worry I know you think your show won't be a success, but I will do all the work and I assure you will have a great show! Now which date is better _____or _____?

Cindy: Well, I guess I can have a show how about _____date. Now, I am not promising you a lot of people or sales?

IHSC: Oh don't worry, I don't expect you to do my job, I will just ask one thing from you and that is to complete a guest list, I will do everything else to ensure the show is a success and to show you just how easy and fun it is to be an _____In Home Sales Consultant.

Cindy: Ok, We will see!

Whatever the response is have your recruits to WRITE IT DOWN Using a Lead Tracking System AND teach them to FOLLOW-UP! Prospects will do something each day. They will either buy, book a show, request to be placed on your call backlist, or maybe even inquire about becoming a consultant.

CHAPTER 9
DON'T PUT ALL YOUR EGGS
IN
ONE BASKET

One of the hardest lessons I have had to learn as a Network Marketer striving to work smart not hard was not to put all of my eggs in one basket.

Early on in my network marketing career I worked with a company that unfortunately went belly up, leaving my million dollar sales organization and me high and dry.

And it's equally important to mention here that while Milton and I successfully opened the doors for many African American artists and their works and enabled thousands of consultants earn extra income, prizes, trips and awards, it came at an enormous price and sacrifice.

When large box companies such as Wal-Mart and K-Mart got into the game of marketing African American works, our network marketing company was simply not able to compete with the big box companies as the larger retailers were able to market artists' works at a significantly reduced price. Hence, unfortunately, we had sales consultants who worked smart and hard for our company also lose their entire sales organizations.

So my friends I have been on both sides of the network marketing company fence, the sales and the company side, hence, I feel confident that I am qualified to advise you,

"DON'T put all of Your Eggs in One Basket."

Network marketing companies have great intentions but they are just like any other business, some will make it and some will fail. Some will conduct great business practice and some will not.

Reflecting on my early days operating in the Network Marketing Industry, I realize some of my greatest obstacles and challenges was due to my inability to focus on the right entity, I was too focused and too loyal to the company's suppliers and its products when truth of the matter is that I should have focused 100% loyalty and attention to our customer base and to organization members or now-a-days called "business partners". As a Network Marketer working smart I encourage you learn the game early on, you can get new product suppliers a lot easier than you get new people.

You see, I had to learn that my business focus as a Network Marketer is not any one company's product, my primary business focus is "People."

I learned that my customers will always be my customers because they trust and believe that if they tell me what they want, I will go out and find for them the best quality products at a very competitive price. They also trust me to deliver and deliver on time.

I further learned that I do not have to worry so much about chasing people around to become one of my network marketing business partners as long as I service my customers in such a way that they WANT to associate with me and if I network to help enough people get what they want, I can have anything I want.

The most important lesson learned was that I never again want to be on either side of the of a losing table:

A business partner who loses a million dollar down-line

Nor

A Direct Sales Company owner who has to file bankrupt and disappoint consultants who will lose a million dollar down-line.

Either scenario sucks!!!

For years I thought my answer was to give up completely on Network Marketing, but clearly that answer did not sit too well with me because once you become successful at Network Marketing you realize that there is NOTHING else like it in the market place.

So what was the answer?

The answer for me was to ensure that I could offer my customers ANYTHING they needed no matter what they asked for. So now, I team up with Direct Sales, Internet Marketing, Online Marketing and Product Brokerage companies that can help me deliver what I need to deliver to my customers and if my customers elect to do what I do then and only then will I introduce them to the supplier of their choice.

This is also a secret that Network Marketers working smart not hard don't share:

Most successful network marketers working smart not hard are involved with two or more direct sales companies simultaneously.

Some would say this is unethical, I would call this smart!

Now before we move forward let me include this statement:

Important note: NEVER mention nor present competing products from different companies during an In-Home party presentation or public event. In fact you should not mention your other company product line(s) at all if it does not come up while you are finalizing individual sales or at the very end of the party after all sales have been complete.

You may feel like contacting them at a later date is an extra step, it is but, Never Ever hang banners or sell products from two different companies at the same time especially at public events. First it is extremely unprofessional, unethical and may just get you terminated from one or both of your companies.

While it is not unlawful to be affiliated with more than one direct sales company at a time and you are certainly an independent business owner, most companies have a clause in your contract that clearly prohibits you from marketing their products alongside their competitors or soliciting distributors to work for their competitors, (read the fine print of your distributor contract before you sign with another company)

While I am in total agreement that one should never market two direct sales companies' products in the same space. I have learned that it is absolutely crazy to leave any money on the table.

Let's take the case of my daughter, Tarin:

Tarin is affiliated with two network-marketing companies right now,

Total Life Change (gotlcdiet.com/tarinboone)

And

Market America (marketamerica.com/tarinboone)

Market America is a Product Brokerage and Internet Marketing Company that has five different divisions by which its distributors can elect to focus. Tarin's focus with Market America is Motives Make-UP.

At the same time, Tarin, is also an independent distributor for Total Life Change her focus with TLC is their weight loss division, specifically, its daily detox system . Tarin became affiliated with TLC because she realized while conducting makeup home parties many women consistently talked about their need to lose weight. Tarin realized she was leaving money on the table.

Realizing that there are thousands of weight lost products and programs on the market including one that Market

America promotes, Tarin did research on the internet to see what women were demanding and what was trending because if she knew what the demand was she knew she could move the product. Her research led her to TLC.

Hence, she became an independent distributor with TLC not because she had intended to start another sales organization, she became affiliated with TLC to fill her customer demand. She has no intentions of recruiting Market America Distributors to TLC and vice versa, however she does plan to share this customer with each company. For instance her weight loss customer will now become customer of Market America who offers millions of products, including non competing great weight loss products. This represents an example of working smart not hard as a network marketer.

I am NOT advocating for anyone to be disrespectful, nor deceitful and attempt to use one organization to build another. Nor am I an advocate for marketing products from two different companies in the same space, this will not benefit you or your organization in the long run. However, focusing on building a lasting relationship with your customer is going to demand that you be able to diversify your product portfolio and offerings based on the customer needs and wants vs. the company's limited product offerings.

Now, if by chance that customer should want to become a consultant for that particular company, well that's what I call working smart? Not only are you retailing products to your existing customer base, you are networking to expand your residual income opportunities between both companies sharing that same customer.

I am not sure why many CEO's of network marketing companies are so opposed to this share of customer mentality, it is my thought that it is better to keep a distributor in some capacity than lose them totally. I have seen several network marketing companies lose entire organizations because of their rigid standards against non-competing companies and or products.

I also feel that some companies use double standards when it comes to the supplier network marketing company sharing it's products with other sales, advertising and distribution companies'. With the onset of online marketing, retailing and affiliate marketing channels , I am sure that there are very few network marketing companies out there operating solely via the use of independent distributors. Hence, one could argue that that some network marketing companies are their distributors biggest competitors???

I feel like this, its not personal its business. I don't have a problem with companies utilizing other channels to move their products, in return, I expect the companies that I partner, not to have a problem with me "not putting all my eggs in one basket," again its not personal its business!

Many ask, how you juggle being affiliated with more than one network marketing company and my response is this:

"The sales are going to be the sales, I have learned how to follow and proven plan or action and have become a master at listening. Every day I listen to what people are talking about all around me, waiting to hear what someone mentions they want or need, and when I hear those magic words, I offer solutions, that's how I move product. Because people have different needs an desires I associate myself into companies that will allow me to help prospects and customers get what they want.

In addition, several people are interested in learning how to build two different organizations simultaneously.

The answer is quite simple. Keep them separate and each focused on moving product. If you do this, the organizations will grow themselves organically, the key is to keep each organization focused on moving product not recruiting.

As far as building different organizations, I balance how much time I am going to spend on organization building based on the performance of each company.

I view each company as a separate business unit within my company, If one company's organization is performing at a far better pace than the other, that is the organization I place most of my recruiting focus on, again its not personal its business.

If one of my business units is operating in the red or simply not growing , I do not just leave the company and customer high and dry. In any retail business you are developing , you will have some business units that will perform better than others, which does not mean that you throw the other business unit out the door, especially after you have invested in them. I remain with companies as long as I have a customer base and there is a demand for their product. After 24 mos. I determine, the extent by which I continue to participate (time-energy-effort) in each business unit based on my company's ROI from that unit at the end of the Two year period.

Thus it is crucial that I make sure that I connect with the right companies that allow me to offer my customers products that are trending and in great demand. In addition I make sure that I am partnering with a company that is offering me the best possible ROI for my investment into their company.

Yes, you are an investor in any network marketing company that you connect to. Make no mistake about it, the company cannot maintain multi-million dollar enterprises without you (the investor) bringing your customers (assets) to the table consistently.

Customer Retention

If you are primarily a jewelry consultant and your clients are talking about weight loss, it only makes sense for you to partner with a weight loss company to be able to satisfy your jewelry clients down the road does it not? Now you have two reasons to stay in touch with that client to purchase more jewelry.

If you are a makeup advisor and someone is asking about tires, it only makes sense to learn more about becoming a Market America Personal Shop Consultant does it not?

Example:

You are a conducting a makeup party in your hostess home, you have completed the presentation and you are writing up your final sale, during that time that guest mentions that she has been having problems with her car and fears that she will have to buy a battery for her car.

After you complete your sale and thank her for the purchase, you advise her that you are also a personal shop consultant and you can assist her purchasing a battery online at a drastically reduced cost and if she is interested you can send her a link a little later that evening.

The guest advises you that she is very appreciative of your gesture and will look to receive the E-mail that evening.

You continue finalizing your sales and another guests walks into the room and thanks the hostess for the dessert offering and makes mention that she really has to lose weight—you in turn advise her, with other the ladies in the room listening, that you are a also a personal shop consultant and that you found a tea that allows you to detox every day and helps you to lose weight in fact many of your clients lose up to 5 pounds in five days.

Suddenly everyone in the room wants more information, you advise them that you will be happy to forward all of them information a little later that evening.

You are now packing up your car the hostess comes out and ask you for more information about becoming a consultant.

You get it!

Bottom line,

If you want to become a Network Marketer that works smart and not hard you must transform your thinking from "company loyalty" to "people loyalty."

Currently, while I am no longer an In Home Sales Consultant, I am a Network Marketer working smart that connects as a distributor, affiliate or strong advocate for direct sales companies, here are two of my favorites:

Traci-Lynn Jewelry: I am not a consultant of Traci –Lynn Jewelry but I am a very strong advocate for this company and refer a LOT of people to join her organization, why you may ask? While I have no financial interest in Traci Lynn Jewelry, I have watched in awe, this American based network marketing company build their organization from a small start-up to an extremely successful international network marketing firm with its focus being a very niche market—jewelry! I also love the fact that allegedly this organization will allow its consultants to be affiliated with other non-competing companies-- with restrictions of course. (An attribute that very few American based Network Marketing Companies will allow)

I personally will not involve myself with any network marketing company who absolutely restricts my ability to market non competing products from other companies to my customer base, remember I am an investor in my suppliers distribution company and I bring the greatest asset to them, My customer base, not theirs. Just as I have to respect my supplier company's distribution strategies, I only want to work with companies who understand my sales strategies.

YOU GET IT!

One of my favorite affiliations with Market America-A product brokerage and internet marketing company: A few paragraphs back I mentioned a young lady noting at a make-up party that she needed to buy battery for her car. That was a true story that happened to my daughter.

At the conclusion of my daughter's make up party she went home signed onto her Market America sponsored website and sent her new friend a link to the page where her new friend (customer) could buy the battery. Her new customer was quite impressed not only was she able to purchase the battery at a much cheaper price, she also received cash back off the sale, my daughter will earn cash back and guess what, so will I, guess who signed my daughter up to be a distributor with Market America?

What I love about being affiliated with Market America internet sales division is that there is no mandatory stocking of inventory, everything is drop shipped, my customers get cash back, and it fits like a glove into my business bottom line of being able to offer customers everything. Ok, I would not be considered a smart Network Marketer If I did not place a plug here: To learn more about its offerings and becoming a business partner visit: http://marketamerica.com/glendaboone

Now, would Market America prefer I focus solely on Market America, I don't know the answer to that question but I am almost sure every network marketing company would desire its distributors to focus 100% on their company's offerings, however, is that a smart business practice for me to take as a Network Marketer working smart and not hard, I don't think so.

There is one other area by which I am a very strong advocate, affiliate network marketing, for more information on this sleeper please visit my blog at: http://www.glendaboonethemuse.com

By connecting myself to these areas I am able to work smart not hard as a network marketer and ensure my company's growth for years.

At the end of the day my friends, we are business owners and we have to always focus on OUR organization's bottom line. Putting all your eggs in one basket in this industry is risky to say the least.

I know that I am going against the grain of what many direct sales company owners would want me to say and what they would want you to read but I am being transparent and speaking from experience.

"DO NOT PUT ALL YOUR EGGS IN ONE BASKET!"

There are thousands of direct sales opportunities and companies for you and members of your organization to become affiliated. find the one(s) that works for you and build on it using the examples I outlined above.

As a Network Marketer working smart I elect and recommend focus on three areas to move product and build a successful network marketing organization:

- Beauty & Fashion

- Health

- Affiliate Network/Internet marketing

Why these three areas?

Because that is what customers are demanding and the way people are shopping. Remember, we only build successful large organizations when we are able to move a lot of product. If you would like some recommendations based on the above categories please visit my website http://www.glendaboone.com and subscribe to my mailing list.

CONCLUSION

Your sales are reflective of what you create!

Your recruits are reflective of the time and money that you are willing to invest in them!

If you really want to make a full time career as a Net Work Marketer and want to work smart and not hard, you must become a master at creating the ultimate in home party/show/presentation and maintain the passion, drive and determination to duplicate yourself with recruits.

If you learn to master these two items, you WILL Succeed. Some will succeed faster than others based on their personal passion but each person will succeed. For the only way that you will fail, is if you become inpatient, refuse to follow the proven plan of action and/or QUIT!

I trust that you are not a quitter because you have purchased this book,

Hence, Stop Crying and Start Building

Get busy booking in home parties and recruiting prospects so that you can move forward in living the life you **WANT** to live.

Best of Luck to you and I look forward to meeting you at the TOP!

ABOUT THE AUTHOR

Glenda Boone has established herself as a successful business owner, coach, proficient manager of entertainment related venues and a muse to CEO's pastors and artists across the country.

As a 20 year veteran of entertainment business management opportunities, Ms. Boone, well-known by African American Artists as "their muse" is recognized for being the first African American Female to establish an In Home Direct Sales Art Marketing firm showcasing the works of hundreds of contemporary African American Artists.

In her own words:

"I am a child of God, wife, mother and marketer I am inspired to get what I want in life by helping enough people get what they want! What do you want and how may I "The Muse" help you?

To request a public appearance by Mrs. Boone to conduct an onsite training seminar or motivational speech to your organization, please forward a written request stating all details including time date and to info@glendaboone.com or by visiting her website at www.glendaboone.com. Check out www.glendaboonethemuse.com for network marketing tips.